Happy Mother's Day!

Presented to:

_____

Presented by:

_____

Date:

_____

Happy Mother's Day!

Honor Books
Tulsa, Oklahoma

Fourth printing

Happy Mother's Day!
ISBN 1-56292-782-5
Copyright © 2000 by Honor Books
P.O. Box 55388
Tulsa, OK 74155

Written and compiled by Sarah M. Hupp.

Introduction

Can you stir a pot on the stove, balance a baby on your hip, hold a telephone at your ear and a toddler on your knee—all at the same time? Are you the person for whom the members of your family yell when they can't find their shoes, socks, homework, or keys; when they need an errand run; when the dog must be walked; or when a shirt needs to be ironed? If so, the evidence points to the fact that you're probably a mother, stepmom, adopted mother, mother-in-law, grandmother, or great-grandmother.

We've put together this collection of inspirational and heartwarming Mother's Day poems, trivia, traditions, Scriptures, and other interesting facts about your day. So sit back and relax (even if you need to hide out for a while) and know that you are loved. And most of all—have a happy Mother's Day!

Happy Mother's Day

For encouragement in tough times,
For laughter amid tears;
For teaching me so many things
I've remembered through the years.

For all the love you've given;
For all the kisses too;
For all these things and many more,
I send my thanks to you.

And on this day so special
I send this poem your way;
With lots of love I wish you
A Happy Mother's Day!

—SARAH MICHAELS

Did You Know?

Mother's Day was instituted officially on May 9, 1914, when President Woodrow Wilson proclaimed the day as a "public expression of our love and reverence for the mothers of our country." In signing a joint resolution of Congress, President Wilson recommended that Congress and the executive departments of the federal government observe this special day to honor all of the mothers in our nation. The following year, President Wilson was authorized by Congress to proclaim Mother's Day as an annual national holiday.

A Mother's Day Tradition

The carnation is the traditional flower of Mother's Day. The House of Representatives voted in 1913 to request that the President, his cabinet, members of Congress, and other government officials wear a white carnation on Mother's Day. Over the years, the carnation has remained the favorite flower for Mother's Day. Tradition now dictates, however, that white carnations honor mothers who are deceased, whereas red or pink carnations signify that the wearer's mother is still living.

Mothers are like fine collectibles—
as the years go by they increase in value.

Do not despise your mother when she is old.
—PROVERBS 23:22

All that I am, or hope to be,
I owe to my angel mother.
—ABRAHAM LINCOLN

Abraham Lincoln's natural mother (Nancy Hanks Lincoln) died when he was nine years old. Lincoln's father remarried, and Sarah Bush Johnston Lincoln became Abraham's stepmother. As Abraham Lincoln grew older, his memory of his natural mother dimmed as his love and respect for his stepmother grew. In later years, he referred to his stepmother, who filled his heart with love, as his "angel mother."[1]

A Special Way to Celebrate

It's Mother's Day—and mothers are the center of attention!
So celebrate your day in a special way. Choose a favorite hat or
have your children make one for you. Tuck a feather in the
hatband or glue some shiny beads or bangles on the brim. Be
prepared to wear it all day—outside in the yard, at mealtimes,
even when leaning across the fence to talk to a neighbor. And
if someone asks about the hat . . . tell them it's your crown!
For today you are royalty—you are queen for a day!
Celebrate—with a hat!

*My sainted mother taught me a devotion
to God and a love of country which
have ever sustained me in my many
lonely and bitter moments of decision
in distant and hostile lands. To her,
I yield anew a son's reverent thanks.*[2]

—GENERAL DOUGLAS MACARTHUR

I looked on child rearing not only as a work of love and duty but as a profession that was fully as interesting and challenging as any honorable profession in the world and one that demanded the best that I could bring to it.

—ROSE FITZGERALD KENNEDY

Heartfelt Expressions of Love for My Mom

A mother is a mother still,
The holiest thing alive.[3]

—SAMUEL COLERIDGE

Blessed are the mothers of the earth.
They combine the practical and spiritual
into the workable ways of human life.[4]

—WILLIAM L. STINGER

She gets up while it is still dark . . .
and her lamp does not go out at night.

—PROVERBS 31:15,18

Did You Know?

- Mother's Day is the busiest day for restaurants in the United States, with the majority of people eating out at lunchtime.
- Mother's Day is also the third-largest card-selling holiday, with 147,000,000 cards being mailed last year, according to the folks at Hallmark Cards.
- And, Mother's Day accounts for the fourth-largest volume of long-distance telephone calls placed in one day, surpassed only by Christmas, New Year's, and Thanksgiving.

A Mother's Day Tradition

Different families observe different traditions during Mother's Day. Some bring mom breakfast in bed. Some go to church together. Some fix all of mom's favorite meals. Some write songs and stories and draw pictures for their mothers. Some take their moms to a favorite museum or park. And some families even let their moms decide what they want to do for the day. If you don't have a tradition for Mother's Day, why not start one this year?

The Hand That Rocks the Cradle

They say that man is mighty,
He governs land and sea,
He wields a mighty scepter
O'er lesser powers that be;
But a mightier power and stronger
Man from his throne has hurled,
For the hand that rocks the cradle
Is the hand that rules the world.[5]

—WILLIAM ROSS WALLACE

*A mother is a blend of strength
and survivorship, experience and
insight, fancy and reflection.*

*Take the word "family." Strike out the
"m" for mother and "y" for youth—
and all you have left is "fail."*[6]
—OMAR BURLESON

*She watches over the affairs of her household
and does not eat the bread of idleness.*
—PROVERBS 31:27

A Special Way to Celebrate

How many times has a mother heard, "Mom, there's nothing to do!"? Don't let Mother's Day be one of those "nothing-to-do" days. Here are some suggestions to help make this Mother's Day memorable:

- Make reservations at a local restaurant for a special brunch.
- Visit a local museum or art gallery.
- Pack a picnic lunch and take a bike ride through a beautiful park.
- Shop 'til you drop at that specialty store you've always wanted to visit (If the family goes along, they have to promise to behave and not complain!).
- Have available all of the ingredients for your favorite dish. Let your family do the cooking and cleanup.

A mother is the truest friend we have, when trials, heavy and sudden, fall upon us; when adversity takes the place of prosperity; when friends who rejoice with us in our sunshine desert us when troubles thicken around us, still will she cling to us, and endeavor by her kind precepts and counsels to dissipate the clouds of darkness, and cause peace to return to our hearts.[7]

—WASHINGTON IRVING

*Motherhood. A chance born of ourselves; a gift given
to ourselves. A serious teacher of unselfish sacrifice. Being forced to
peek in the mirror of our own human frailties. Having to wear the
yoke of responsibility while trying to look graceful, unruffled,
knowledgeable. Having a sense of humor when we know we aren't
humorous. Realizing that one good moment
can erase about one hundred bad ones.
Yes, motherhood: remembering the days
may be long, but the years are short.*[8]

—BETH LAZAR

An ounce of a mother's wisdom
is worth a pound of psychiatry.

A mother needs fortitude and courage and tolerance and flexibility
and patience and firmness and
nearly every other brave aspect of the human soul.
But because I happen to be a parent of almost
fiercely maternal nature, I praise casualness.
It seems to me the rarest of virtues.[9]

—PHYLLIS MCGINLEY

A woman who fears the LORD is to be praised.

—PROVERBS 31:30

'Tis Mother's Day

I'm sitting on the front porch
In my favorite rocking chair;
My daughters hover over me
With gentleness and care.

My feet are on a pillow;
My glass is filled with tea.
My every wish is their command—
'Tis Mother's Day, you see.

I wish this day would never end—
A selfish wish I guess.
But when the sun goes down, you see,
I'll have to clean the mess.[10]

—BEV QUADE

Did You Know?

During the 1600s, many of England's poor worked as servants on the estates of wealthy landowners. On the fourth Sunday of Lent, servants were given the day off and were encouraged to go home and spend the day with their mothers. This annual holiday became known as "Mothering Sunday." In some areas of England, children brought bunches of primroses or narcissus as tokens of their affection. A special cake, called a mothering cake, was also often brought along to provide a festive touch for the occasion.

A Mother's Day Tradition

Mother's Day in America is observed on the second Sunday in May. Many Mother's Day traditions center around the church. Some Christians bring flowers to the altars of the church where they were baptized. Some churches line the altar with colorful potted flowers, such as geraniums, and deliver the bright blooms to aged mothers who can no longer attend church. Still other churches grant special recognition to the oldest and youngest mothers in the congregation. Many churches also sponsor Mother/Daughter dinners and outings at this same time of year as another way of honoring mothers.

M-O-T-H-E-R

"M" is for the million things she gave me,
"O" means only that she's growing old;
"T" is for the tears were shed to save me,
"H" is for her heart of purest gold;
"E" is for her eyes, with love-light shining,
"R" means right, and right she'll always be,
Put them all together, they spell "MOTHER,"
A word that means the world to me.[11]

There are only two lasting bequests
we can hope to give our children.
One is roots; the other, wings.

—HODDING CARTER

*The only mothers it is safe to forget
on Mother's Day are the good ones.*[12]

—MIGNON MCLAUGHLIN

*Love is patient, love is kind. It does not envy,
it does not boast, it is not proud. It is not rude,
it is not self-seeking, it is not easily angered,
it keeps no record of wrongs.*

—1 CORINTHIANS 13:4–5

A Special Way to Celebrate

Mother's Day can be a time to send greetings to grandmothers, aunts, mothers-in-law, and anyone who has ever been or even wished to be "mommified." During the week prior to Mother's Day, announce to your children that the special day is approaching. Gather some construction paper, a baking cup, glue, crayons, and a picture of your child. Using the baking cup as a flower blossom, cut out leaves and a stem from green construction paper. Glue the child's picture inside the blossom. Glue the stem, leaves, and flower to another piece of paper and add a crayoned message.

*The mother's heart is
the child's schoolroom.*[15]

—HENRY WARD BEECHER

We all too seldom put in words
Our thoughts from day to day;
About how much we value those
Who've loved us on the way.
So this is just to let you know
What's now and always true—
All the best that "Mother" means to me
Is wrapped up tight in you.
Happy Mother's Day!

—CONOVER SWOFFORD

Lessons from Mom

My mother taught me a multitude of virtues simply through the example of her life. She taught me how to befriend and care for people who are less fortunate, yet be able to mingle in the most elite settings. She demonstrated to me that a true and loving smile can win over the hardest of hearts. As I get older, I realize that her greatest lessons of all I learned not from what she said, but by her knowing when to be silent.

—SHARON K. RICKARD

And the Lord Created . . . Mothers

When the Good Lord was creating Mothers . . . an angel appeared and said, "You're doing a lot of fiddling around on this one."

And the Lord said, "Have you read the specifications on this order? She has to be completely washable, but not plastic; have 180 movable parts—all replaceable; run on black coffee and leftovers; have a lap that disappears when she stands up, a kiss that can cure anything from a broken leg to a disappointed love affair, and six pairs of hands. . . ."

Youth fades, love droops,
the leaves of friendship fall;
a mother's secret hope outlives them all.

—RALPH WALDO EMERSON

A Mother's Day Tradition

Mother's Day is a worthy holiday for both mothers and their children. On this holiday, we hear kind remarks addressed to those mothers still living and glowing eulogies of mothers who have passed away. For centuries in England, it has been customary to place complimentary remarks on the tombstone of any mother who has died during the previous year. These remarks are traditionally inscribed prior to Mother's Day so that all who visit the churchyard on that day will be able to read the words and share in the sentiment.

There is no velvet so soft as a mother's lap
no rose as lovely as her smile,
no path so flowery as that
imprinted with her footsteps.

—ARCHIBALD THOMPSON

Heartfelt Expressions of Love for My Mom

*Throughout the ages no nation has
ever had a better friend than the mother
who taught her children to pray.*[13]

Her children arise and called her blessed.

—PROVERBS 31:28

*Fortunate woman! My children
usually arise and call me, "Ma!"*[14]

—JEAN E. SYSWERDA

A Special Way to Celebrate

Create a memory on Mother's Day! Purchase a plain T-shirt or sweatshirt in your favorite color and a tube of fabric paint in a complementary color (white paint on dark shirts or dark-colored paint on light shirts works best). Place some of the fabric paint on a heavy, coated paper plate. Thin the paint with a little water. Have each special person in your family place their hand, palm side down, in the paint and "stamp" their handprint on your shirt. When hands are washed and the shirt has dried, you'll have a visual memory of this special day!

*A mother is a person who seeing there
are only four pieces of pie for five people,
promptly announces she never did care for pie.*

—TENNEVA JORDAN

*Whatever you do, work at it with all
your heart, as working for the Lord.*

—COLOSSIANS 3:23

A Mother's Prayer

Help me, dear Lord, to be a good mother . . .
To guide those depending on me.
Help me to show them a mother whose love
And purpose is centered on Thee.

Let them see kindness and wisdom enough
To teach them the worthier things . . .
Patience enough to encourage their hearts
To love life, whatever it brings.

Let me inspire them to look for—and find—
The best in themselves and each other . . .
How grateful I'd be if they lived well for Thee
In faith that they learned from their mother.[15]

—D. A. MARCUM

Every Day Is Mother's Day

The most glorious occasions of my career weren't nearly as sweet as simple moments I've spent with my family. Being a mother is a strange job. There are no paychecks, promotions, days off, or fresh salads for lunch. Day in and day out, it's a vocation that's wonderful, horrible, rewarding, thankless, challenging, and tedious. And while the routine can leave moms drained from head to toe, their hearts are always filled with pride, guilt, and love.[16]

—JANET KONTTINEN

*By and large, mothers and
housewives are the only workers
who do not have regular time off.*[17]
—ANNE MORROW LINDBERGH

*Whatever you do, whether in word or
deed, do it all in the name of the Lord Jesus,
giving thanks to God the Father through him.*
—COLOSSIANS 3:17

You never know what gifts you give a mother will bring the most enjoyment. Friends of a young mother with three young children were surprised when they received the following thank-you note: "Many thanks for the playpen. It is being used every day. From 2-3 P.M., I get in it to read, and the children can't get near me."[18]

Did You Know?

Four years prior to its becoming a national holiday, Mother's Day was first officially celebrated in West Virginia in 1910. Oklahoma followed this example in 1911. By 1912, the Mother's Day International Association came into existence, and the majority of states celebrated Mother's Day in some way. Some celebrated in May, while others celebrated in June. Also in 1912, Governor Hay of Washington asked his people to attend church and to visit or write to their mothers on this holiday, or to wear white carnations if their mothers were no longer living.

A Mother's Day Tradition

Although the celebration of Mother's Day at first was carried out only in church programs, the scope of the holiday's observance has broadened to include other demonstrations of affection such as gifts, letters, and visits. Telegraph companies, florists, candy companies, and card makers keep a steady stream of advertisements flowing through television, radio, and print media to encourage retail sales at this time. Their advertising blitz must be effective: in 1991, more than seventy-five million families bought Mother's Day gifts, totaling more than $987,000,000.

Only a Mother Knows

The tenderness of her newborn babe
With all its precious charms;
The motherly love beyond compare
For the baby in her arms.

The wonderful feeling of joy and pride
With her little one cuddling close;
The heavenly joy of a baby near,
Only a mother knows.[19]

—JOY BELLE BURGESS

*Automation is a process that gets
all the work done while you just
stand there. When we were younger,
this process was called MOTHER.*[20]

*Make it your ambition to lead a quiet life,
to mind your own business and to work with
your hands, just as we told you, so that your
daily life may win the respect of outsiders.*

—1 THESSALONIANS 4:11–12

A Special Way to Celebrate

Find a photo booth in a mall or shopping center that takes a series of photos and immediately processes them. Squeeze as many family members as you can into the photo booth and make silly and serious faces for each of the photos. Glue these instant prints to the front of a colorful Mother's Day card. Ask each member in the photo to autograph the collage. Purchase a picture frame in which the recipient can display the card as a reminder of the special day.

*The heart of a mother is a deep abyss
at the bottom of which you
will always find forgiveness.*[21]

—HONORÉ DE BALZAC

*My mother was the most beautiful woman
I ever saw. All I am I owe to my mother. I attribute all my
success in life to the moral, intellectual,
and physical education I received from her.*[22]

—GEORGE WASHINGTON

Tell Mother I'll Be There

When I was but a little child how well I recollect
How I would grieve my mother with my folly and neglect;
But now that she has gone to heav'n I miss her tender care:
O Savior, tell my mother, I'll be there!

Tell mother I'll be there in answer to her prayer,
This message, blessed Savior, to her bear!
Tell mother I'll be there, heav'n's joys with her to share,
Yes, tell my darling mother I'll be there.[23]

—CHARLES M. FILLMORE

Even He that died for us upon the cross,
in the last hour, in the unutterable agony of death,
was mindful of His mother, as if to teach us
that this holy love should be our last worldly
thought—the last point of earth from which
the soul should take its flight for heaven.[24]

—HENRY WADSWORTH LONGFELLOW

Who takes the child by the hand
takes the mother by the heart.[25]

—GERMAN PROVERB

See that you do not look down on one of these
little ones. For I tell you that their angels in
heaven always see the face of my Father in heaven.

—MATTHEW 18:10

Put Your Feet Up

A tired mom was standing by the sink after supper on Mother's Day, facing a mountain of dirty dishes and greasy pots and pans. Her eldest daughter was clearing the dining-room table and saw her mother surveying the mess. As the older woman began to roll up her sleeves, her daughter quickly stepped to her side and put her arm around her mother's shoulder. "Mom," she said, "it's Mother's Day. You shouldn't have to do these dishes." As the weary mother turned to thank her daughter for her willingness to tackle the monstrous chore, her daughter interrupted, saying, "Go, put your feet up. You can finish these dishes tomorrow!"

Did You Know?

In 1907, two years after her own mother's death, Anna M. Jarvis began a letter-writing campaign to influential businessmen, clergymen, and members of Congress, asking them to establish a special day to honor mothers. Anna Jarvis persuaded the Andrews Methodist Church in Grafton, West Virginia, to hold a special Mother's Day service on May 10, 1908, to honor Anna's mother, who had taught Sunday school classes in the Grafton church for more than twenty years. On that same day, six years before the national recognition of Mother's Day, a similar service honoring mothers was held in Anna's church in Philadelphia.

A Mother's Day Tradition

I think everything alive longs for love and attention, and the more love we give to our gardens, the more they give back to us. No geraniums blossomed more beautifully or grew more profusely than those on my Mama's windowsill.

Her friends used to say to her, "Maria, how can your geraniums blossom like that all the time?"

Mama used to smile happily and reply, "That is because I talk to them!"

So on Mother's Day, I practice Mama's method—and it always works.[26]

—THYRA FERRÉ BJORN

I have worshipped in churches and chapels;
I've prayed in the busy street;
I have sought my God and have found Him
Where the waves of His ocean beat;
I have knelt in the silent forest
In the shade of some ancient tree;
But the dearest of all my altars
Was raised at my mother's knee.[27]

—JOHN H. STYLES JR.

The joys of motherhood are never fully experienced until all the children are in bed.[28]

She sets about her work vigorously; her arms are strong for her tasks. She sees that her trading is profitable, and her lamp does not go out at night.

—PROVERBS 31:17-18

A Special Way to Celebrate

You deserve a day to relax! So why not pamper yourself on Mother's Day. Ask your children to prepare a bubble bath fit for a queen. Assemble whatever lotions, perfumes, or bath oils you might have on hand. Grab a cold drink and a favorite book or one you've wanted to read but just haven't had the time for. So that there will be no unwanted interruptions, make sure all the other family members are not going to need to use the bathroom for a while. Then settle back for an hour or so and soak away your cares.

My mother said to me,
"If you become a soldier you'll be a general;
if you become a monk you'll end up as the pope."
Instead, I became a painter and wound up as Picasso.

—PABLO PICASSO

The hunger for love is
much more difficult to remove
than the hunger for bread.

—MOTHER TERESA

*A mother's love is indeed the golden link
that binds youth to age; and he is still but
a child, however time may have furrowed his
cheek, or silvered his brow, who can yet recall,
with a softened heart, the fond devotion, or
the gentle chidings, of the best friend
that God ever gives us.*[29]

—CHRISTIAN NESTELL BOVEE

There is a vast difference between seeing our children just as our children and seeing them as our disciples. If they're just our children, then our only concerns are . . . to feed and clothe them, get them into the right schools, well married, etc. But if they're also our disciples, then, more than anyone else, within those twenty or so precious years we have them, we're to teach them everything Jesus has taught us.[30]

—ANNE ORTLUND

Train a child in the way he should go, and when he is old he will not turn from it.

—PROVERBS 22:6

Now who would let you use her sewing machine
to make doll clothes and get things all out of place?

And who would let you mix up cookies when you
spilled sugar on the floor and got flour on everything?

And who could fry the most delicious chicken and
would save your favorite piece for your school lunch?

And who would warm an old flat iron and
wrap it in towels so it would warm
your cold bed and not burn you?

My Mom

—CLEO JUSTUS

Did You Know?

Mother's Day is observed in many countries around the world. Denmark, Finland, Italy, Turkey, Australia, and Belgium celebrate Mother's Day on the second Sunday in May, just as we do in the United States. England, China, India, Sweden, and Mexico honor mothers on the fourth Sunday in Lent. And the Slavic countries tie their Mother's Day celebrations to the Christmas season, honoring mothers at the beginning of Advent.

The Sounds of Mother's Day

A mixer whirs out of control, then stops abruptly as a voice cries, "I'm telling." A dog barks and another voice says, "Get his paws out of there. Mom has to eat that!" Minutes pass, and finally, "Dad! Where's the chili sauce?" Then, just before the food is served you hear, "Don't you dare bleed on Mom's breakfast!"[31]

Sweetest of Mothers

Sweetest of Mothers; whate'er betide
You are patience personified.
Never a sign of complaint on your face,
Accepting God's will with such sweetness and grace.

No words I could utter would ever express
The praise you deserve. No look or caress
Of mine ever show, the love in my heart
For you, my dear mother, when near or apart.

When God takes you from me and closes your eyes
And your spirit is wafted beyond through the skies
Oh, Lord, give me courage and faith then to say
Thy will and not mine, be done on that day.[32]

—LOTTA B. MILLER
(Written for her mother, Hanna Blackburn,
on the occasion of Mother's Day, 1914.)

Heartfelt Expressions of Love for My Mom

*A mother's kindly deeds are only seeds of love
to help her children grow in the garden of life.*

*Maternal love: a miraculous substance,
which God multiplies as He divides it.*[33]

—VICTOR HUGO

*As God's chosen people, holy and dearly loved,
clothe yourselves with compassion, kindness,
humility, gentleness and patience.*

—COLOSSIANS 3:12

A Special Way to Celebrate

Do you save old greeting cards? If you do, take some time today to select a favorite Mother's Day or birthday card that you received from your child. Find a special frame for the card and hang the card someplace where you will see it often. Every time you look at the card, you'll give a boost to your self-esteem and reinforce your child's self-confidence and assurance of your love, too.

Love: A Variation on a Theme

If I live in a house of spotless beauty with everything
    in its place, but have not love,
I am a housekeeper—not a homemaker.
If I have time for washing, polishing, and decorative
    achievement, but have not love,
My children will learn of cleanliness—not godliness.
Love leaves the dust in search of a child's laugh. . . .

. . . Love picks up the child
before it picks up the toys. . . .
Love reprimands, reproves, and is responsive. . . .
Love is the key that opens
salvation's message to a child's heart.
Before I became a mother I took
glory in my house of perfection.
Now I glory in God's perfection of my child.
As a mother there is much I must teach my child,
But the greatest of all is love.[34]

—JOANN MERRELL

*A mother understands
what a child does not say.*

—JEWISH PROVERB

*Cleaning your house while your kids
are still growing is like shoveling
the walk before it stops snowing.*[35]

—PHYLLIS DILLER

*Teach us to number our days aright,
that we may gain a heart of wisdom.*

—PSALM 90:12

*Life is not a matter of milestones,
but of moments.*

—ROSE FITZGERALD KENNEDY

Like kites without strings
And butterfly wings,
My mother taught me
To soar with my dreams.

—WILLIAM H. McMURRY III

Did You Know?

After the Civil War, officials in Taylor County, West Virginia, brought peace to the Union and Confederate families in their area by hosting a "Mother's Friendship Day" program. One woman dressed in gray and another woman dressed in blue asked the band to play "Dixie" and "The Star Spangled Banner" and urged the celebrants to sing along. The two ladies then urged the celebrants to shake hands while the band played "Should Auld Acquaintance Be Forgot." When the song ended, everyone was weeping and shaking hands. In the audience was a young girl, Anna Jarvis, the future founder of Mother's Day.[36]

A Mother's Day Tradition

On the first official Mother's Day service on May 10, 1908, Anna Jarvis sent five hundred white carnations to the Andrews Methodist Church in Grafton, West Virginia. She asked everyone to wear this flower because "it may be thought to typify some of the virtues of motherhood; . . . whiteness stands for purity; its lasting qualities, faithfulness; its fragrance, love; its wide field of growth, charity; and its form, beauty." The following year, seven hundred carnations were sent for the same purpose. Until her death, Anna Jarvis maintained this tradition and sent over ten thousand carnations as personal gifts to the Andrews Church.

God made a wonderful mother,
A mother who never grows old,
He made her smile of the sunshine,
And molded her heart of pure gold!
In her eyes He placed shining stars,
In her cheeks, fair roses you see,
God made a wonderful mother,
And gave that dear mother to me.[37]

—PAT O'REILLY

God pardons like a mother who kisses
the offense into everlasting forgetfulness.[38]

—HENRY WARD BEECHER

The LORD is compassionate and gracious,
slow to anger, abounding in love. He will not
always accuse, nor will he harbor his anger
forever; he does not treat us as our sins deserve
or repay us according to our iniquities.

—PSALM 103:8–10

A Special Way to Celebrate

Take some time on Mother's Day to play! If you have to stay inside because of bad weather, have a bubble-gum blowing contest with your children or grandchildren. Who can blow the biggest bubble? Who can make their bubble last the longest? If the weather is nice, find some sidewalk chalk and draw silly pictures and messages of love on your front walk or driveway. Encourage everyone to participate. But whether you can play indoors or out, make sure that you have plenty of laughter, hugs, and fun.

Heartfelt Expressions of Love for My Mom

No one on this earth could ever take her place,
Not even stately queens dressed in gold and lace.

She was a simple lady with good old fashioned ways,
And warm homemade bread made for happy summer days.

I remember her love for God, saw her kneel in prayer,
She told me Bible stories and what was good and fair.

She made my favorite foods, soup when I had the bug,
She cleaned my skinned-up knees and healed them with a hug.

—CLEO JUSTUS

A Legend of Love

One day a baby was snatched from its crib by a gigantic eagle and taken to the top of a nearby cliff. Several strong men tried to rescue the child, but they all failed. A woman glanced upward and began to scale the cliff. Step by careful step she made it to the top. While the onlookers watched, the woman cautiously climbed down the cliff with the baby until she stood safely at the bottom. Why did she succeed when others had failed? She was the baby's mother, and nothing is as courageous as a mother's love.

The size of the problem reflects the size of the child;
when the child is small, the problems are small; when
the child gets larger, so do the problems. But a mother
need never fear the future—for God is already there.

My times are in your hands.

—PSALM 31:15

When I was small you took my hand—
Before we'd walk across the street,
Before you'd tuck me into bed,
Before the blessing for each meal,
Before I left for school each day.

Now I've grown and you take my heart—
Every step I go,
Every place I stay,
Every meal I prepare,
Every job I do.

You've held me—hand and heart—for so long
Through hard times,
Through growing times,
Through good times,
Through in-between times.

And now I hold you, in my heart, with love.
Happy Mother's Day.

—S.M.H.

Did You Know?

Julia Ward Howe, the author of "The Battle Hymn of the Republic," was one of the first persons to promote the idea of Mother's Day. During the Civil War, she suggested that July fourth be set aside as a holiday devoted to peace and recognized as Mother's Day. Her proposal was rejected in favor of continuing to celebrate our national independence on that date.

A Mother's Day Tradition

Before the official adoption of Mother's Day as a national holiday, the people of Henderson, Kentucky, maintained a tradition of holding a musical program in honor of the mothers in their community. Mary Towles Sasseen, a teacher in the public-school system, spent a great deal of her time organizing this yearly event in the late 1880s. The program was held in the local school, and the pupils' mothers were invited to attend. As the music festival gained in popularity, neighboring schools and localities were also included in the planning and presentations.

Women know
The way to rear up children
(to be just)
They know a simple, merry, tender knack
Of tying sashes, fitting baby-shoes
And stringing pretty words that make no sense.

—ELIZABETH BARRETT BROWNING

*A mother knits the family together with the threads of honor
and respect, weaves their lives together with nurture and care,
and holds them all tightly with bonds of love and prayer.*

*Good deeds are obvious, and even
those that are not cannot be hidden.*

—1 TIMOTHY 5:25

*A mother's lap is the best place
from which to launch a life.*

A Special Way to Celebrate

Build a fort! Remember the joy small children have in building a fort from couch cushions and card tables? Enlist the aid of your little architects and build a fort fit for a mom. Use couch cushions, blankets, a card table, or whatever else you have on hand. Make sure your fort is comfortable and big enough for you and a few guests. You may want to position a window or doorway in the fort so that you can recline and view a favorite video or television program while you munch popcorn and relax.

Most of all the other beautiful things in life
come by twos and threes, by dozens and hundreds.
Plenty of roses, stars, sunsets, rainbows, brothers and sisters,
aunts and cousins, but only one mother in the whole world.

—KATE DOUGLAS WIGGIN

Protect her life, I pray,
Who gave the gift of life to me;
And may she know,
From day to day,
The deepening glow
Of joy that comes from Thee.

I cannot pay my debt
For all the love that she has given;
But Thou, love's Lord,
Wilt not forget
Her due reward,—
Bless her in earth and heaven.[39]

—HENRY VAN DYKE

There is only one pretty child in the world,
and every mother has it.

—ENGLISH PROVERB

*Whatever you would have your children
become, strive to exhibit in your
own lives and conversation.*[40]

—LYDIA H. SIGOURNEY

*Train a child in the way he should go, and
when he is old he will not depart from it.*

—PROVERBS 22:6

*Remember:
a mother is not merely someone to lean on,
but someone who makes leaning unnecessary.*

Heartfelt Expressions of Love for My Mom

*There was never a great man
who had not a great mother.*

—OLIVE SCHREINER

Did You Know?

For many years, people urged the Postmaster General to issue a stamp honoring Mother's Day. In 1934, James A. Farley ordered a three-cent stamp featuring a painting called *Arrangement in Black and Grey*. Known more commonly as *A Portrait of Whistler's Mother*, this painting embodied the spirit of motherhood and became a distinctive stamp that was welcomed all over the United States. The original portrait was ultimately purchased by the French government and exhibited at the Chicago World's Fair in 1934.

A Mother's Day Tradition

Some churches follow the tradition of setting aside the entire month of May as a time to honor mothers. Mothers fill the roll as greeters, ushers, and soloists. Sermons throughout the month highlight different mothers in the Bible, including the familiar (Sarah, Naomi, Mary, and Elizabeth) as well as the obscure (Bilhah, Zipporah, and Zelophehad's wife). On Mother's Day, the men of the congregation take care of all of the setup and cleanup for the day as well as care for the nurseries during Sunday school and worship services.

What Is a Mother?

A mother is someone who shelters and guides us,
Who loves us, whatever we do,
With warm understanding and infinite patience
And wonderful gentleness, too.

The heart of a mother is filled with forgiveness
For any mistake, big or small.
She's generous always in helping her family,
Whose needs she has placed above all.

A mother possesses incredible wisdom
And marvelous insight and skill.
In each human heart is that one special corner
Which only a mother can fill![41]

—KATHERINE NELSON DAVIS

*Who is best taught? He who has
first learned from his mother.*[42]

—THE TALMUD

*She speaks with wisdom, and
faithful instruction is on her tongue.*

—PROVERBS 31:26

*True mother-love never fails to point
her child to the Author of Love.*[43]

—SUSAN L. LENZKES

A Special Way to Celebrate

Take some time on Mother's Day to make a Mom's Timeline—a visual reminder of special events, transitions, hard times, and good times that highlight God's presence in your life as a mom. Use materials you have on hand—poster board and paints, stickers and a blank book, colorful trims or buttons on a quilt square, paper clips or safety pins on a bulletin board, or draw small stick figures or sketches in an art pad to record those special events. Continue to add to this timeline throughout the year and find a deeper sense of God's care in your life.

*Kind words are short and easy to speak,
but their echoes are truly endless.*

—MOTHER TERESA

*Mother means selfless devotion, limitless sacrifice,
and love that passes understanding.*

*Motherhood is a
partnership with God.*

Over my slumbers your loving watch keep;
Rock me to sleep, mother; rock me to sleep.[44]

—ELIZABETH CHASE

He will not let your foot slip—he who watches
over you will not slumber. The LORD will
keep you from all harm—he will watch over
your life; the LORD will watch over your
coming and going both now and forevermore.

—PSALM 121:3,7-8

Thank you for tucking me in bed at night.
Thank you for leaving the door open for light.
Thank you for hugging away every fright.
Thank you, dear Mother, thank you.

Thank you for washing my hands and my feet.
Thank you for cooking my favorites to eat.
Thank you for always being proud of me.
Thank you, dear Mother, thank you.

Thank you for teaching and loving and then
Thank you for doing it all over again.
Thank you, dear Mother, for all you have been.
Thank you, dear Mother, for you.

—S.M.H.

Did You Know?

In the middle 1930s a group in New Mexico tried to interest the nation in a celebration for mothers-in-law. While a few civic groups in the southwest responded to this idea and sponsored some events honoring mothers-in-law, the idea was soon abandoned. Both mothers and mothers-in-law are now recognized on the second Sunday in May, on Mother's Day. Greeting card companies also include "Happy Mother's Day, Mother-in-law" cards in their holiday assortment.

The Things I'm Thankful for on Mother's Day

I'm thankful that . . .

Mom let me sleep late on weekends.

Mom made my favorite supper and dessert for my birthday.

Mom reminded me to wear my best underwear in case I
    got into an accident and had to go to the hospital.

Mom taught me to use a tissue instead of my sleeve.

Mom changed my diapers, no matter how messy.

Mom rocked me in the rocker even when
    I was too big to sit on her lap.

Mom read me my favorite story—over and over and over again.

Mom let me keep pets, even though she had to take care of them.

Mom prayed with me and taught me how to pray.

Mom loved me and taught me how to love others.

The mother-child relationship is paradoxical.
It requires the most intense love on the mother's side, yet this very
love must help the child grow away
from the mother and to become fully independent.[45]

—ERICH FROMM

Do not forget the things your eyes have seen or let them
slip from your heart as long as you live. Teach them
to your children and to their children after them.

—DEUTERONOMY 4:9

A Special Way to Celebrate

Before you go to bed on Mother's Day, go outside and look up at the stars. Lie on your back on a blanket and see which constellations you recognize. Find the brightest star. Look for the smallest one. See if you can play "connect the dots" with the stars. Then remind yourself of these words: "Lift your eyes and look to the heavens: Who created all these? He who brings out the starry host one by one, and calls them each by name. Because of his great power and mighty strength, not one of them is missing" (Isaiah 40:26).

Looking forward to the time when my earthly career will end, I desire to set forth at the very beginning of this will, as the most important item in it, a confession of my faith in Jesus Christ as my Savior. I also desire to bear witness to the fact that throughout my life, in which there were unusual joys and sorrows, I have been wonderfully sustained by my faith in God through Jesus Christ. This legacy was left me by my consecrated mother, a woman of strong faith, and to it I attribute any success I have attained.[46]

—FROM THE WILL OF HENRY J. HEINZ

My daughter's first home of her own . . .

When I arrived for my overnight visit, the towels
lay on the bed just the way I always put them out
for her on trips home. She served me a cold drink.
Offered me a snack. Made me feel at home in her home.
It was like watching a movie of myself. Our visit was short,
but we covered a lifetime of memories. And now, heading out
the door, I again feel the hug she gave me earlier. I take it
with me as I leave her home—and head for mine.[47]

—LISBETH J. THORN

*Mother: The name for God in the
lips and hearts of little children.*[48]
—WILLIAM MAKEPEACE THACKERAY

*Your inner self, the unfading beauty of a gentle and
quiet spirit, . . . is of great worth in God's sight.*
—1 PETER 3:4

*A mother is the one through whom
God whispers love to His little children.*

Definitions From a Mom's Perspective

Panic: What a Mom goes through when the baby's wind-up swing stops.

Walls: A complete set of drawing paper for the kids that comes with every room.

Terrible Twos: Having both kids home all summer.

Quiet: A state of household serenity which occurs before the birth of the first child and again after the last child has left for college.[49]

Did You Know?

The founder of Mother's Day, Anna Jarvis, spent many years and much of her fortune promoting the celebration of the holiday. But when Mother's Day became a national holiday, Miss Jarvis was greatly disturbed by the commercialization that accompanied it. For the remainder of her life, Miss Jarvis attempted to reverse this exploitation, speaking at church and school gatherings and writing to businessmen and politicians, urging her listeners to remember the original purpose of Mother's Day: to show honor and gratitude to those who gave us birth.

A Special Way to Celebrate

A Mother's Day breakfast in bed is fairly traditional: a water tumbler of orange juice, half a dozen pieces of blackened bacon, enough scrambled eggs to feed a boy scout troop, and three pieces of cold, over-buttered toast. Your children stand by the bed to watch you eat and ask if you need another napkin or if the food is to your liking. On Mother's Day, your children give rather than receive, and offer you the sincerest compliment they can extend: trying to do for you what you do for them every other day of the year.

My Dear Mother

Who taught me how to read and write?
Who doctored my mosquito bites?
Who calls me on the phone each night?
My Mother.

Who taught me how to tie my shoe?
Who still knows fun things we can do?
Who always says, "I love you, too"?
My Mother.

Who taught me that it's best to share?
Who keeps me in her thoughts and prayers?
Who always loves and always cares?
My dear Mother.

—SARAH MICHAELS

*A wise mother knows that her children
rely more on her example than on her words.*

*Follow my example,
as I follow the example of Christ.*
—1 CORINTHIANS 11:1

*The deepest fountains of love are found
at the cross of Christ and in a mother's heart.*

*My mother gave me the example of the completely dedicated
life. In my father, this was translated
into action, and in my mother into silence.
We all live from what woman
has taught us of the sublime.*[50]

—POPE PAUL VI

A Special Way to Remember

Why not keep some of the wishes you receive this year for a "Mother's Day Time Capsule." Save greeting cards, notes, poems, and photographs. Keep them in a special envelope or box, and tie it with a colorful ribbon. Tuck this "time capsule" away in the back of your closet or under your bed to be retrieved at a much later date. Such a collection will be a blessing to you and your children in later years—a true treasure trove of love.

Did You Know?

When Anna Jarvis sought to establish a Mother's Day observation, most of her appeals fell on deaf ears. It wasn't until she spoke to John Wanamaker, the great merchant and philanthropist from Philadelphia, that the movement gained momentum. Mr. Wanamaker presided over a Mother's Day service held in his store's auditorium on May 10, 1908. The auditorium had a capacity of five thousand, but more than fifteen thousand sought entrance. Anna Jarvis was the guest speaker, and she held her audience spellbound for over an hour. The occasion was a great success—both for the Mother's Day movement and for Wanamaker's.

What a mother sings to her children
follows them all the way through life.

Physical training is of some value, but godliness
has value for all things, holding promise for
both the present life and the life to come.
—1 TIMOTHY 4:8

A mother renders matchless service
to humanity in every field of life.

While helping her grandmother move to a smaller residence, a young woman stumbled across some of her grandmother's personal correspondence. Stored for years in an old filing cabinet, this unexpected find yielded a rare glimpse of the love shared between her mother, grandmother, and great-grandmother in the form of touching letters, heartfelt wishes, and ardent poetry.

Tucked into one envelope was this letter, written by her own mother:

Dear Mother and Grandmother,

I am writing this letter to tell you how I appreciate all you have done for me. Sometimes you think I am just awful, I know, because you have to scold me, and I am ashamed of myself. You just don't know how much I appreciate the things you've done for me.

Your loving daughter,
"Bits" (11 years old)
May 8, 1936

Penned on the back of the letter, in girlish script, a Mother's Day rhyme:

> I hold you dearest mother mine
> From all the world apart;
> Thoughts of your goodness softly shine
> Like sunlight in my heart;
> Truest friend above all others
> Gentlest, kindest, best of mothers.
> I love you.[51]

—MARY LOUISE DITTRICK

A Mother's Day Tradition

Some families have two sets of dishes—one for everyday use, and one for special occasions. Mother's Day is a special occasion that calls for the "good" dishes. A beautiful table is set with fresh table linens, cut flowers, candles, and all the special dishes used to honor guests. Do you have this tradition in your home? While the children are still young, you may want to use only certain pieces. But if your children are older, why not enjoy *all* of the "good" dishes. It may even make your Mother's Day dinner taste better than last year's!

A Recipe for a Loving Mother

Take a large bowl of grace. Sprinkle with kindness. Add a dash of smiles and a heap of love. Throw in a dash of forgiveness and a splash of gentleness for flavor. Stir together throughout the years. Serves innumerable children.

—STEPHANIE MICHELE

Of all the rights of women,
the greatest is to be a mother.
—LIN YUTANG

Train the younger women to love their husbands
and children, to be self-controlled and pure, to be
busy at home, to be kind, and to be subject to their
husbands, so that no one will malign the word of God.
—TITUS 2:4–5

A Special Way to Celebrate

It's Mother's Day—let your imagination go! Grab your children or grandchildren and find a sunny spot with a few trees. Spread a blanket on the ground under one of the trees so that you are partially shielded from the sun. Lie on the blanket and look up into the sky. Study the clouds. Find a cloud that could have a "silver lining." Use your imagination and find "cloud pictures" of animals, people, and objects. But be careful. You might be so relaxed after looking at the clouds, that you might . . . feel . . . a little . . . sleepy.

*I attribute my discovery of my heavenly Father largely to
what I had known of the goodness
of my earthly parents. . . . Of religious teaching we had but
little, but of religious example
and influence we had a never-failing supply.
Not by talking, but by daily living, were impressions made
on our childish hearts.*[52]

—HANNAH WHITALL SMITH

No ordinary work done by a man is either
as hard or as responsible as the work of
a woman who is bringing up a family of
small children; for upon her time and strength demands are
made not only every hour of
the day but often every hour of the night.[53]

—MRS. THEODORE ROOSEVELT

Heartfelt Expressions of Love for My Mom

*A man never sees all that his mother
has been to him until it is too late.*[54]

—WILLIAM DEAN HOWELLS

*Near the cross of Jesus stood his mother. . . .
When Jesus saw his mother there, and the disciple
whom he loved standing nearby, he said to his
mother, "Dear woman, here is your son," and
to the disciple, "Here is your mother." From
that time on, this disciple took her into his home.*

—JOHN 19:25–27

My mom is the one I love best
My mom isn't like all the rest
She's fun and she's pretty
She's kind and she's witty
I love you! You are the sweetest!
Happy Mother's Day!

Did You Know?

The Congressional Record of May 8, 1914, contains the account of the passage of the Mother's Day Bill in Congress, setting the second Sunday in May as the official day for the observation of Mother's Day. This bill also authorizes and requires the President of the United States to request this holiday's observance by calling for the display of the American flag on all U.S. government buildings, homes, and other suitable places as a public acknowledgment that the "American mother is the greatest source of the country's strength and inspiration."

A man's work is from to sun to sun,
but a mother's work is never done.

Mother's Love

Mother's love is a precious thing
That deepens through the years,
In memory of bright sunshine days,
Of laughter, love, and tears.

Mother's love is a treasured thing;
Though far from home we roam,
The cherished bonds of faith and love
Still pull our hearts toward home.[55]

—ELISABETH WEAVER WINSTEAD

*A smile is a curve that can
set a lot of things straight.*

*Hannah said to him: "I am the woman who stood
here beside you praying to the LORD. I prayed for
this child, and the LORD has granted me what
I asked of him. So now I give him to the LORD.
For his whole life he will be given over to the LORD."*

—1 SAMUEL 1:26–28

A Special Way to Celebrate

The old cliché says: "A picture is worth a thousand words." On Mother's Day, why not gather the family around your collection of photo albums. Show them their baby pictures. Let the children see what you looked like when you got married. Remember the picnics and family vacations. Compare the family traits: Who has Grandpa's eyes? Who has Grandma's smile? Make sure to take time for love, laughter, and plenty of remembrances as you make a new Mother's Day memory.

*Not until I became a mother did I understand
how much my mother had sacrificed for me.
Not until I became a mother did I feel how hurt
my mother was when I disobeyed. Not until I
became a mother did I know how proud my mother
was when I achieved. Not until I became a mother
did I realize how much my mother loves me.*[56]

—VICTORIA FARNSWORTH

A Mother's Prayer

I am a mother
Called to serve with a grace
That God's love alone conveys.
Lord, give me strength to speak with wisdom.
Lord, give me courage to tell of Your love.
Lord, grant me Your mercy that I might be
A mother who follows Your ways.

*The heart of a mother is a deep abyss at the bottom
of which you will always find forgiveness.*

—HONORÉ DE BALZAC

*A mother's gift is always the best because it's wrapped in love
and tied up with heartstrings.*

*He went down to Nazareth with them and
was obedient to them. But his mother treasured all
these things in her heart. And Jesus grew in wisdom
and stature, and in favor with God and men.*

—LUKE 2:51–52

Who ran to help me when I fell,
And would some pretty story tell,
Or kiss the place to make it well?
My mother.

Who taught my infant lips to pray,
To love God's holy Word and day,
And walk in wisdom's pleasant way?
My mother.[57]

—JANE TAYLOR

Did You Know?

The first Mother's Day in 1908, celebrated at Grafton, West Virginia, was opened with a telegram from Anna Jarvis that defined the purpose of the day: "Mother's Day is to remind us of our duty before it is too late. It is to revive the dormant filial love and gratitude we owe to those who gave us birth. To obliterate family estrangement. To make us better children by getting us closer to the hearts of our good mothers. To have them know we appreciate them, though we do not show it as often as we ought."[58]

A Mother's Day Tradition

In late April and early May, the fields of a nursery and landscape service in central New York State overflow with pansies. This particular nursery works with area scout troops to provide thousands of pansies for distribution to area churches on Mother's Day. Each woman in attendance carries home one of these perky biennials and is encouraged to plant the pansy as a continual reminder of a child's love. Several homes in the area have gardens filled with purple, blue, white, yellow, and bicolor pansy faces obtained over the years because of this nursery's annual tradition.

What are Raphael's madonnas
but the shadow of a mother's love,
fixed in permanent outline forever?[59]

—T.W. HIGGINSON

The angel said to her, "Do not be afraid,
Mary, you have found favor with God.
You will be with child and give birth to a son,
and you are to give him the name Jesus."

—LUKE 1:30–31

A Special Way to Celebrate

Make some Mother's Day resolutions—special things you will do on Mother's Day. Remember, it is Mother's Day, so don't be too hard on yourself. Here are a few suggestions. On Mother's Day I resolve to:

- Get up and eat.
- Postpone one chore for one more week.
- Close the door on my child's messy room.
- Take a shower.
- Pet the dog.
- Throw something away.
- Hug a family member.
- Know that God loves me.

Before you were conceived I wanted you
Before you were born I loved you
Before you were here an hour I would die for you
This is the miracle of life.

—MAUREEN HAWKINS

The successful mother, the mother who does her part in rearing and training aright the boys and girls who are to be the men and women of the next generation, is of greater use to the community, and occupies, if she only would realize it, a more honorable as well as a more important position than any man in it. The mother is the one supreme asset of the national life. She is more important, by far, than the successful statesman or businessman or artist or scientist.[60]

—THEODORE ROOSEVELT

Heartfelt Expressions of Love for My Mom

A mother's patience is like a tube of toothpaste—
it's never quite gone.

Judicious mothers will always keep in mind
that they are the first book read, and the
last put aside, in every child's library.[61]

—C. LENOX REDMOND

In everything set them an example
by doing what is good.

—TITUS 2:7

My mother is my mentor:
Someone who speaks her mind.
She always helps
And gives her best
But says no words unkind.

I hope one day to follow
The steps my mom has trod;
To always help
And give my best
And live my life for God.

—STEPHANIE (AGE 12)

A mother is the one who is still there when everyone else has deserted you.

*The reason that some mothers get along better
in this life is because they have learned to be
kinder than necessary to all who need it.*

*Be kind and compassionate to one another, forgiving
each other, just as in Christ God forgave you.*
—EPHESIANS 4:32

A Special Way to Celebrate

Gather your children together during a quiet moment on Mother's Day and share how each child became a member of the family. Recall the events surrounding each one's birth or the cravings that you developed during your pregnancy. If you have adopted children, share with them the excitement of their arrival and the way you felt when you were told to come and pick them up. If you have stepchildren, recall for them the moment you fell in love with each one. Let your children ask questions, and use this time to reinforce your love for each child.

*Motherhood is the keystone of
the arch of matrimonial happiness.*[62]
—THOMAS JEFFERSON

*When it was time for Elizabeth to have
her baby, she gave birth to a son. Her neighbors
and relatives heard that the Lord had shown
her great mercy, and they shared her joy.*

—LUKE 1:57–58

Every mother is like Moses.
She does not enter the promised land.
She prepares a world she will not see.

—POPE PAUL VI

She has the beauty of a spring day, the patience of a saint, the appetite of a small bird, and the memory of a large elephant. She knows the lowest prices, everybody's birthday, what you should be doing, and all your secret thoughts. She is always straightening up after, reminding you to, and taking care of, but never asking for. And when you have tried her patience and worn her out, you can win her back with four little words, "Mom, I love you!"[63]

—WILLIAM A. GREENBAUM II

Endnotes

[1] Adapted from *Respectfully Quoted: A Dictionary of Quotations,* edited by Suzy Platt. (New York: Barnes and Noble Books, 1993).

[2] *Knight's Treasury of 2,000 Illustrations,* Walter B. Knight. (Grand Rapids, MI: Wm. B. Eerdmans Publishing Co., 1963).

[3] *The Public Speaker's Treasure Chest,* Herbert V. Prochnow and Herbert V. Prochnow, Jr. (New York: Harper and Row, Publishers, Inc., 1977).

[4] *The Forbes Books of Business Quotations,* edited by Ted Goodman. (New York: Black Dog and Leventhal Publishers, Inc., 1997).

[5] *The Harper Book of American Quotations,* edited by Gorton Carruth. (New York: Carruth and Ehrlich Books, Inc., 1988).

[6] *The Forbes Books of Business Quotations,* edited by Ted Goodman. (New York: Black Dog and Leventhal Publishers, Inc., 1997).

[7] *A Dictionary of Illustrations,* by James C. Hefley. Grand Rapids, MI: Zondervan Publishing House, 1971).

[8] Mother's Day contest winners, 1998, CNN Interactive.

[9] *Contemporary Quotations,* compiled by James B. Simpson. (New York: Thomas Y. Crowell Company, 1964).

[10] *Mother's Day Ideals,* edited by Lisa C. Ragan. (Nashville, TN: Ideals Publications, Inc., 1998).

[11] Words by Howard Johnson, music by Theodore Morse. ©1915, renewed 1943 Leo Feist, Inc. Rights assigned to CBS Catalogue Partnership. All rights controlled and administered by CBS Feist Catalog, Inc. All rights reserved. International copyright secured. Used by permission. Taken from *Respectfully Quoted: A Dictionary of Quotations,* edited by Suzy Platt. (New York: Barnes and Noble Books, 1993).

[12] *The Forbes Books of Business Quotations,* edited by Ted Goodman. (New York: Black Dog and Leventhal Publishers, Inc., 1997).

[13] *14,000 Quips and Quotes for Writers and Speakers,* E.C. McKenzie. (Avenel, NJ: Wings Books, distributed by Random House by arrangement with Baker Book House, 1980).

[14] *Women's Devotional Bible 2.* (Grand Rapids, MI: Zondervan Publishing House, 1995).

[15] *Happy Mother, Happy Child: A Guide to Child Care,* Nancy Moore Thurmond. (Wheaton, IL: Tyndale House Publishers, Inc., 1982).

[16] "The Bay Area Traveler Magazine," San Francisco Chronicle, May 4, 1998.

[17] *The Harper Book of American Quotations,* edited by Gorton Carruth. (New York: Carruth and Erlich Books, Inc., 1988).

[18] *1001 Humorous Illustrations for Public Speaking,* Michael Hodgin. (Grand Rapids, MI: Zondervan Publishing House, 1994).

[19] *The Best of Ideals: The Best of Mother's Day.* (Nashville, TN: Ideals Publishing Corp., 1989).

[20] *14,000 Quips and Quotes for Writers and Speakers,* E.C. McKenzie. (Avenel, NJ: Wings Books, distributed by Random House by arrangement with Baker Book House, 1980).

[21-22] Both quotes taken from an online source: http://www.coos.or.us/~dust/mother.htm The Stock Solution, "Special Feature for Mother's Day", May, 1998.

[23] "The Watchman-Examiner" (a Sunday school newsletter), May 1949.

[24] *12,000 Religious Quotations,* edited by Frank S. Mead. (Grand Rapids, MI: Baker Book House, 1989).

[25] *The Harper Book of Quotations,* edited by Robert Fitzhenry. (New York: Harper Perennial, 1993).

[26] *The Home Has a Heart,* Thyra Ferré Bjorn. (Old Tappan, NJ: Fleming H. Revell Co., 1968).

[27] *Masterpieces of Religious Verse,* edited by James Dalton Morrison. (New York: Harper & Row, 1948).

[28] *14,000 Quips and Quotes for Writers and Speakers,* E.C. McKenzie. (Avenel, NJ: Wings Books, distributed by Random House by arrangement with Baker Book House, 1980).

[29] *12,000 Religious Quotations,* edited by Frank S. Mead. (Grand Rapids, MI: Baker Book House, 1989).

[30] *Disciplines of the Beautiful Woman,* Anne Ortlund. (Waco, TX: Word Books Publisher. Proven Word, 1984).

[31] *1001 Humorous Illustrations for Public Speaking,* Michael Hodgin. (Grand Rapids, MI: Zondervan Publishing House, 1994).

[32] From the collection of Claire Miller Dittrick Elly. Used by permission.

[33] *12,000 Religious Quotations,* edited by Frank S. Mead. (Grand Rapids, MI: Baker Book House, 1989).

[34] *Motherhood,* by Barbara Johnson. (Dallas, TX: Word Publishing Co., 1994).

[35] *The Harper Book of American Quotations,* edited by Gorton Carruth. (New York: Carruth and Erlich Books, Inc., 1988).

[36]Adapted from *Mother's Day: A History of Its Founding and Its Founder,* Norman F. Kendall, (published 1937). Online source: http://www.rootsweb.com/~wvtaylor/mother.htm.

[37]*Knight's Treasury of 2,000 Illustrations,* Walter B. Knight. (Grand Rapids, MI: Wm. B. Eerdmans Publishing Co., 1963).

[38]*12,000 Religious Quotations,* edited by Frank S. Mead. (Grand Rapids, MI: Baker Book House, 1989).

[39]*Masterpieces of Religious Verse,* edited by James Dalton Morrison. (New York: Harper & Row, 1948).

[40]*The Harper Book of Quotations,* edited by Robert Fitzhenry. (New York: Harper Perennial, 1993).

[41]Online source: http//www.gentle.org/adonai/happy.html.

[42]*12,000 Religious Quotations,* edited by Frank S. Mead. (Grand Rapids, MI: Baker Book House, 1989).

[43]*When the Handwriting on the Wall Is in Brown Crayon,* Susan L. Lenzkes. (Grand Rapids, MI: Zondervan Publishing House, 1981).

[44]*The Public Speaker's Treasure Chest,* Herbert V. Prochnow and Herbert V. Prochnow, Jr. (New York: Harper & Row, 1977).

[45]*The Harper Book of Quotations,* edited by Robert Fitzhenry. (New York: Harper Perennial, 1993).

[46]*Illustrations Unlimited,* edited by James S. Hewitt. (Wheaton, IL: Tyndale House Publishers, Inc., 1988).

[47]*The Best of Ideals: The Best of Mother's Day.* (Nashville, TN: Ideals Publishing Corp., 1989).

[48]*A Dictionary of Wit, Wisdom, and Satire,* Herbert V. Prochnow and Herbert V. Prochnow, Jr. (New York: Harper and Brothers, 1962).

[49]Online source: http://www.geocities.com/Heartland/Pointe/5892/Mothersdayrembrances.html.

[50]*For Mom,* compiled by Jennifer Habel. (White Plains, NY: Peter Pauper Press, 1995).

[51]Taken from the personal collection of Claire Miller Dittrick Elly. Used by permission.

[52]*The Women's Devotional Bible 2.* (Grand Rapids, MI: Zondervan Publishing House, 1995).

[53]*For Mom,* compiled by Jennifer Habel. (White Plains, NY: Peter Pauper Press, 1995).

[54]*Who Said That?,* George Sweeting. (Chicago, IL: Moody Press, 1995).

[55]*The Best of Ideals: The Best of Mother's Day.* (Nashville, TN: Ideals Publishing Corp., 1989).

[56]*Illustrations Unlimited,* edited by James S. Hewitt. (Wheaton, IL: Tyndale House Publishers, Inc., 1988).

[57]*Who Said That?,* George Sweeting. (Chicago, IL: Moody Press, 1995).

[58]Online source: http://www.rootsweb.com/~wvtaylor/founder.htm.

[59] *The Public Speaker's Treasure Chest,* Herbert V. Prochnow and Herbert V. Prochnow, Jr. (New York, NY: Harper & Row, 1977).

[60]*Knight's Treasury of 2,000 Illustrations,* Walter B. Knight. (Grand Rapids, MI: Wm. B. Eerdmans Publishing Co., 1963).

[61] *You Can Say That Again,* compiled by R.E.O. White. (Grand Rapids, MI: Zondervan Publishing House, 1991).

[62]*A Dictionary of Wit, Wisdom, and Satire,* Herbert V. Prochnow and Herbert V. Prochnow, Jr. (New York: Harper and Brothers, 1962).

[63] *Who Said That?,* George Sweeting. (Chicago, IL: Moody Press, 1995).

The "Did You Know?" information is adapted from *All About American Holidays,* Maymie R. Krthye. (New York: Harper & Brothers, Publishers, 1962); *The Concise Columbia Encyclopedia, Third Edition;* and online resources, including: http://www.gentle.org/adonai/happy.html.

If you have enjoyed this book, or if it has
impacted your life, we would like to hear from you.
Please contact us at:

Honor Books
Department E
P.O. Box 55388
Tulsa, Oklahoma 74155

Additional copies of this book
are available from your local bookstore.